Like an Ever-rolling Stream

Poems by
Rosemary Parrott

LIKE AN EVER-ROLLING STREAM

Published by Magic Flute Publications 2016
ISBN 978-1-909054-36-3
Copyright © Rosemary Parrott

Rosemary Parrott has asserted her right under the Copyright, Designs and Patents Act 1988 to be identified as the author of this work.
All rights reserved. No part of this publication may be reproduced, stored in a retrieval system, or transmitted in any form or by any means, electronic, mechanical, photocopying, recording or otherwise, without the prior permission of the copyright owner.
All illustrations © Rosemary Parrott

Magic Flute Publications is an imprint of

Magic Flute Artworks Limited

231 Swanwick Lane

Southampton SO31 7GT

www.magicflutepublications.co.uk

A catalogue description of this book is available from the British Library

For Betty
1927-2015

Time, like an ever-rolling stream
bears all our years away;
they fly, forgotten, as a dream
dies at the opening day.

Isaac Watts (1674-1748) altd.

FOREWORD

Time and again well-meaning friends advise: "that's all in the past now, and you must put it behind you."

If only life were that simple! Our present circumstances and outlook are more usually conditioned by past experience, and our future shaped by the consequences of that past, many of them unforeseen and therefore beyond our control.

It is the writer's privilege (and sometimes pain) to inhabit other people's lives, drawing on this fresh narrative to augment limited personal resources. In this respect, radio provides a rich seam of experience: the lady coerced into a career deemed suitable for girls who, rebelling in middle age, took herself off to university and finished up with a PhD in Psychology; the man so deeply scarred in childhood by the insensitivity shown at the death of a parent that he trained as a Family Bereavement Counsellor in the hope of sparing other children similar anguish; some stories are so harrowing that it becomes almost unbearable to listen and it's difficult to envisage how there could be any form of future redemption in the situation.

This collection of poems brings together many such threads, exploring the ways in which the past influences the present while containing the seeds of a future which, if we only knew where to look, is already forming round us.

Rosemary Parrott   April 2016

Contents

ANCESTRY	3
TO AN UNKNOWN GRANDMOTHER	5
LOST LANDSCAPE	7
REVERIE	10
YESTERDAY'S CHILD	11
ERIC'S ROOM	13
PSALMSONG	16
LILAC TIME	18
GRADUATED SCALE	21
OMENS	24
THE WINDMILLS OF MYKONOS	27
FAST FORWARD	29
ARROWHEAD	30
i Prologue	30
ii Attention all Shipping	31
CHILD GRIEVING	49
TO A NEWBORN DAUGHTER	51
ALPHA MALE	53
TO A HARPSICHORD	55
POET BURNING	57
OVERLOAD	59
POND LIFE:	61
i SINE NOMINE	61
ii THE FROG PRINCE	63
TRAIN	66
GIFT DAY	69
DODECANI	71
WHITE HORSES	73
WILD FLOWERS	75
A SONG OF THE WILD	76
SOLSTICE	81

IN SUSPENSO	83
HARD WINTER	85
FLEDGELINGS:	87
i SUMMERHOUSE	87
ii YESTERDAY MORNING	90
SONG FOR ELUNED	92
SPRING CLEAN	94
STAINED GLASS WINDOWS	96
OFFICES	99
HOW FAR IS IT TO BETHLEHEM?	101
THREE SOLILOQUIES	
AT THE FOOT OF THE CROSS:	103
i I AM HIS MOTHER, MARY	103
ii I AM PETER	105
iii I AM MARY	107
HEAVEN IS BUT BEYOND	109

ACKNOWLEDGEMENTS

P. iii. Verse 4 of 'Our God, our help in ages past', Rejoice and Sing, (Oxford: Oxford University Press for the United Reformed Church, 1991)

P. 35. Excerpt from 'Good Friday', Sonata in the Key of Life (Southampton: Magic Flute Publications, 2012)

REVERIE, YESTERDAY MORNING and SONG FOR ELUNED were originally composed as songs, but are included here for their observations, both on some of life's threshold events, as well as those more elusive moments, often so fleeting that they defy identification.

PAST CONTINUOUS

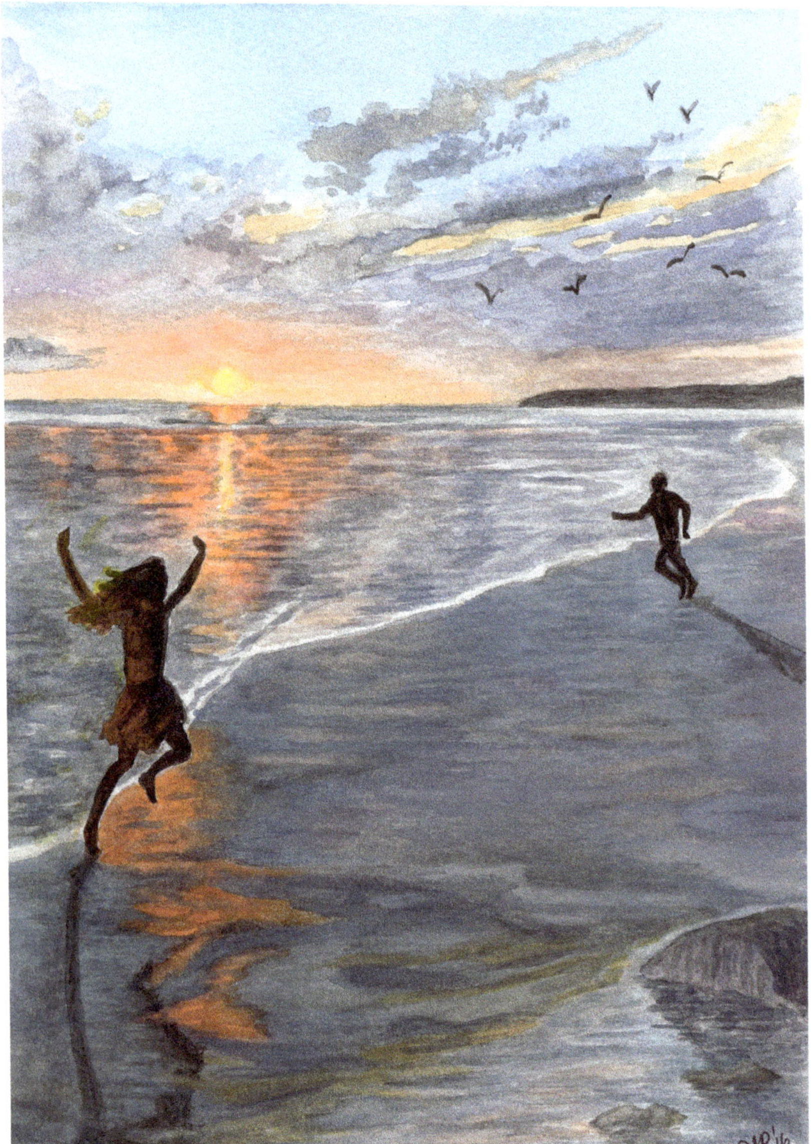
RAP'16

ANCESTRY

'Genes Reunited':
A cupboard door
Once opened,
All the skeletons
Revealed
For evermore:

Fathers who died
Not knowing
Where their children were,
Barred by rancour
Dating back
Fifty years ago
Or more.

Little girls
Brought up by grandmamma,
Their mother – gone,
To seek a new life
On a foreign shore,
Hoping for a chance
To start again.

Violent, drunk
Victorian men,
Each one in turn
Neglected child of
Widowed motherhood,
Left to raise alone
Posthumous sons
Their fathers never knew;

Then add
To this already turgid brew
The ones conceived in secret
Or by accident:
Strange fruit upon
The family tree
Whose origins are
Never truly known;

Let him whose ancestry
Is without fault
Cast the first
Stone.

TO AN UNKNOWN GRANDMOTHER

You gaze across
The newly-found
Family photograph,
The grandmother I never knew,
Your focus somewhere
To the right of camera,
Soft hair ruffled by the breeze
In late spring.

I search your features,
Longing for a hint,
A clue
That something unidentified in me
Might be found
In you;
While in the centre of the group,
Chubby, mop-haired first-born
On her lap,
The last vestige of
My mother's girlhood
Wears my earlier face:
A disconcerting thing.

What occasion
Spurred this moment
We may never know;
But some, no longer recognised,
Choosing to dignify
This memorable day

Ninety years ago
With bow tie, waistcoat, braces,
Floral hat or cap,
The congenial company
Sprawl together on the grass
Beside the sea,

And you,
The matriarch,
My unknown grandmother,
Are now forever in my mind,
Younger than me.

LOST LANDSCAPE

Fermain Bay, 1950

This year's white sandals
  have no T-bar strap
  and when no one is looking
  I walk in them on tiptoe,
  imagining how my feet
  will look when I'm a
  grown-up lady in
  high-heeled shoes.

Ordinarily,
  he would have had to park the van
  outside these
  half-timbered houses where the
  rich people live,
  and carry wooden crates through the
  tradesmen's entrance.
  But on Sundays we are
  people too, and we
  walk down the middle of the empty road
  on the way back to the
  bus stop.

The hedgerow opposite
  has a path worn in the grass,
  and I would love to
  run along the top and
  jump down into the field
  like other children do –
  but I understand that 'they' must see
  I have been taught to behave
  properly.

I remember when I rode shoulder-high
  past tea-room smells of
  hot teapots in wooden baskets,
  and waspclouds round
  sticky ice-cream wrappers, sickly sweet
  booty of brimming–over litter bins;
  winding single file up stone-lined cliff paths,
  ducking low-lying brambles and
  chanting aloud the succession
  of each steep flight of
  concrete steps.

I must plod them wearily myself
  now my mother says I'm old enough,
  wishing I had asked for a
  smaller spade.
  A familiar tickle
  of pink sunburn prickles on my shoulders,
  and toes skid on dry sand in
  gritty shoes.

And as this year's sandals
  have no T-bar strap, so
  jigsaw patterns of light and shade from
  the canopy of trees weave
  right across my feet
  and are left behind
  on the surface of the
  street. Voices
  joined at the elbow for nearly thirty years
  murmur above my head,

Just like last year and the
   year before, and a question
   starts to form wordlessly
   round the edges of my mind:
   this life's-landscape seeming
   oh-so-safe, but O, for how many
   years more?

REVERIE

Here in the dark,
When the first touch of daylight begins
To reveal old familiar things
That my dreaming had
Stolen away,

Memory
Sings to me softly of beautiful things,
Of a hawk that climbed high in the sky
On the wings
Of a warm summer day.

Is there a prayer
For a fragrance that hung in the air,
Leaving traces so faint
I was never quite sure
If it really was there?

YESTERDAY'S CHILD

Since the past crept up on me
And seized me in its grip
I suppose
You had to be the first
To go.
Kind and gentle,
Mindful of my needs
- and a man -
You are everything
That other world
Did not permit.

Watching you
From the far side of the room
As you smile and talk
With people who are
Comfortable to be with you,
I would run to you
And fling my arms around
All that you are. But,
Being heavy-years away
And so far out of reach,
I might as well be
Manacled
And held in chains
Against the wall.

Now I have begun
The long journey
Home from that distant
Country,
Inching my way back towards
The way things are now -
Having always been my friend,
Stand beside me quietly,
Until I can remember
How it feels
To be brave enough
To reach out
And take your hand.

ERIC'S ROOM
Rue Escarpée, Le Havre

She said, apologetically,
"I hope you don't mind –
I've put you on
The children's floor,"
And led me
Up the last flight
Of a spiral staircase,
Through a door
To a maze of attic rooms.

As I lay awake in an
Unfamiliar bed
High above the silent port,
The rising wind
Moaning softly at the
Open window,
Tears came at last,
And I cried into the darkness,
Thinking in French
For the first time in years:
"Eric est mort."

Eric is dead,
His long life's journey at an end,
And his friends have said
That I should come and play for him
For the last time
When he is laid to rest.

The morning curtains opened
On a grey and ragged day,
But when a sickly sun
Had tried its best
To fight its way bravely
Through the weeping sky,
In the deep recesses of the window sill
A printed text within a picture frame,
Attended by
A little wooden Viking man,
Displayed the name
ERIC.

"A name
Of Nordic origin,"
It said,
"Meaning 'son'."
Translating from the French
I read that ERICs are
Full of contrasts:
Brave and gentle,
Strong and sensitive,
And blessed with great finesse,
Which touches
Everything they do.

"Why are you here with me
In a foreign land,
In this house high above the sea?"
I asked my old friend
With the tired, bearded smile,
Still tentatively tapping

With his white cane,
And struggling for breath –
Then, reeling now
At the realising of his death,
I took the words
To show Madame.

"Ah, yes," she said,
"Until the message came
In the afternoon,
I had not been expecting
A third guest,
And so,
As he is away from home
For a while,
I gave you
Eric's room."

A little wooden Viking man displayed the name ERIC

PSALMSONG

They said
"It's time you recognised
And learned to know
Your place.
The pursuit of beauty
Has to be
The preserve
Of those who can aspire
To a higher
Way of life.
There can be no
Creative fire
In the rest."

Then I understood
That for me
There was supposed to be
A lifetime spent,
Nose pressed
Against the window
Of opportunity,
On the outside
Looking in.

But still, the psalmist said[1]
There are no accidents
Of birth,
Each one of us
Lovingly assembled
In a mother's womb
To make a contribution
To the world
Which is unique,
And known
To God alone.

And so I paint my picture,
Sing my song
And weave words into poetry;
And when the Maker of the universe
Summons me
To see if I have
Squandered my inheritance,
I will apologize
That there should be
Such a small return
On the endowment
Of His grace;

But because He loves me,
He will understand
That it might have been
Even less
If I had been content
To know my place.

---

1   Psalm 139.

LILAC TIME

It took three days
To find
A copy of the right music,
So that he could make
His last journey
To the strains
Of his favourite melody.
But here we are,
On course
In the middle of the second verse,
With three minutes left
Before his final entrance:

*"We'll watch without a sigh
The moments speeding by"*

No screech of tyres,
No squeal of brakes,
No warning:
Just a hideous,
Sickening crunch
Dredged up
From the bowels of the earth
And transferred into mine
Through the pedal board
Beneath my feet
And the wooden stool
On which I sit
To play……

......followed by
Not so much a silence
As a suspension of time itself,
Into which still falls
Grotesquely,
Obscenely even,
A song of springtime
In an English lane.

No more gathering lilacs now,
With screaming sirens
And a sudden pandemonium
Outside. But the show
Must go on;
Find something more appropriate
To say:

*"Ave, Ave,
Verum corpus"*

Blue and white tape
Stretched across the door,
And we become not a church
But an extension of a
Crime scene,
Through which yellow vests
And huddled red blankets
Ebb and flow
In slow motion.

"For the Lord
Is mindful of His own"

Cover the giant wheels
To bring some privacy
To the last moment
She didn't know she had.

Eventually,
We are allowed
To gather lilacs
In the spring again,
Although this time
With one more bloom
In our bouquet
Than we had bargained for.

GRADUATED SCALE

Three photographs
Hang upon the wall
Of the piano room,
Graduates all
In cap and gown
And strained smile.

The first
Was taken twenty years ago,
The memento of
A Welsh LanguageFest
Spectacular,
With pageantry of
Mediaeval academic
Dress and
Passionate voices
Raised in song,
Almost drowned
By the swelling sound
Of the organ
In St David's Hall.

The second
Was a more restrained
Affair:
Rows of wooden chairs
Flanked the aisle
In the nave
Of an Anglican
Cathedral.

Proud parents,
Waiting there
To witness the achievements
Of their offspring,
Had to brave instead
An interminable discourse
On the merits
Of the candidate
For an honorary
Doctorate,
Which we thought
Was not entirely
Fair.

The last, most recent,
Was a horse
Of a different feather:
Crammed together
In a tent in Hendon,
Pounding music
Heralded the
Unrestrained,
Whooping, shrieking
Triumph
Of a crop of
New Graduates
In Performing Arts.

In this world apart,
The familiar title of
'Mature Student'
Suddenly becomes
A euphemism
Meaning simply
OLD;
For despite
Being made to wait for it
For nearly fifty years,
When the time for Graduation
Finally arrives
'Mature students'
Sometimes find themselves
Completely out
In the cold.

OMENS

I woke in the half-light
To the sound of
Gulls,
A screeching mass
Erupting upwards into the
Steel-grey dawn,
Tripped, no doubt,
By some private dispute
Over ownership
Of a crust of bread
Or some other juicy find.

And being only half-awake,
In that strange, dream-like state
Which is
Uncertain of reality –
Slowly disengaging from my
Dream cottage in a
Cornish fishing port
And groping my way back
To an existence
Of a more mundane
Suburban sort –

Still steeped in sleep,
I thought:
"This must be an omen
Of some deep impending evil,
Global warming, or a grave
Transgression
Of another kind".

But a bleak day's remembering
Reminded me
That gulls always take refuge
Inland
From stormy weather out
At sea.

More ominous than gulls
For people only half-awake
Is a half-grasp of truths
Disguising
Shadows of the mind.

Houses on Mykonos, Greece

THE WINDMILLS OF MYKONOS

"The art class will convene
In the observation lounge
At 10am". For many
Of the group it was
'Business as usual',
An extension of their
Shore-based class
In Bournemouth,
But for me, it was
A return to painting
For the first time in
Forty years.

To my surprise,
Faced with a blank
Sheet of paper
There was no recourse to the
Blind panic of
Schoolroom days;
Instead, I sat
Happily absorbed,
Painting sea, while
Gazing out across
The straits of Gallipoli.

I need to practise
My techniques, because
We're going to paint the
Windmills
When we get to Mykonos.

Mount Athos was
Majestic,
Skiathos was too rough;
The ship was rolling
Far too much
And things kept
Sliding off the tables
Where we honed our skills
And learned artistic flair –

But when we get to Mykonos
We'll paint the windmills
There.

When we finally arrived
At Mykonos
Our ship was berthed
In the wrong place,
Too far to reach the windmills
In one afternoon,
So we settled on a
Windy promenade
To paint
A red boat with a
White wheelhouse
Against a background of
Houses on a steep hill.

Well, there was
One small windmill
Near the top.

FAST FORWARD

....so, more than
One year later,
Searching in a drawer
To find a
Long-lost sketching-pad,
I unearthed
A painting from my
Teenage years,
Unexpectedly preserved –

A red boat with a
White wheelhouse
Against a background of
Houses on a steep hill:

Arrowhead.

c 1960   *Nestling on her cradle on the Hard.*

ARROWHEAD

i Prologue

On the stroke of eight
By the
Town Church clock
She slips her moorings
In the
Early morning sun.

Seaward bound
On her first cargo run
Of the day
She threads her way
Between the sleeping
White yachts,
Their pyjama'd sailors
Just emerging barefoot
From below,
Blinking in the
Unaccustomed light.

Milk churns from the dairy,
Hampers full of bread,
Feed for the poultry
And a brand new bed.
Spare parts for the tractor,
Mailbag sealed up tight,
This morning's English papers
From the UK flight:
An important factor in
The daily round of
Island life is
Arrowhead.

ii Attention all Shipping

Especially in sea areas
Wight, Portland,
Plymouth, Biscay...

Wind south-west, force 2 to3
1013, steady. Fog at first,
Clearing later.

More sophisticated ships
Equipped with radar
Or with GPS
Slip nonchalant into the fog
And confidently
Hoot their way
To Guernsey.

But smaller fry such as we
Have to creep
Self-consciously
Through the
Damp, white candy-floss,
Perched on our own
Miniscule,
Pewter-grey
Circumference of
Visibility.
Away to port,
Occasionally
A thin, high-pitched
Ghostly sound
Pipes timidly
Into the void,
While on the starboard side
A raucous, rising groan,
Not unlike the bellow
Of a bullock in distress,
Pauses at its height -
Then hits its final bass-note
With a thud.

From time to time
Rocks and reefs
Which line the
Low-tide passages
Show dimly
Through the mist,
But otherwise
We grope our way, until
The sky begins to lift

And we reach the
Pier-head on a
Sparkling summer's day.

Wind south-east
Force 2 to 3; 1026,
Rising slowly;
More than 20 miles.
Deep Low moving in from the
Azores,
Expected North Biscay 1600
GMT

Mountains of menace stack,
Piled sheer above the black land,
While shafts of yellow light
Leer below.
Upon the black patent sea
A tiny, solitary craft creeps home,
A frightened miniature
Caught out,
Alone and vulnerable
On God's table-top
Model of the universe.

The eerie silence snaps:
With rifle crack
A twisted flicker hurtles earthward,
Splitting as it comes.
Against the backdrop of an evil sky
Shocked islands lie impaled
Upon the fork,
Footstools to a quivering arc
Thirty miles wide
And less than half a second high.

For a small eternity
The scene is etched upon unwilling minds
Until the earth
Recoils beneath the first bombardment.
Then the rumbling, tumbling blitz begins,
Cascades of invisible rage,
Battering puny mortals
Into submission.

When skies grow dark out in the street
And hailstones desecrate
The neat, suburban sprawl,
Look back across the years
And contemplate
The horror of it all.

What privilege it was
To see the size and scale
On which the universe is made;
In one split second look upon its face
And know what fragile craft
God's people sail.

Remember then,
When darkness falls at three o'clock
And have the grace
To be afraid.

Wind east-north-east
Veering east by north,
Force 4 to 5, Freshening 5 to 6.
Gales later; 998,
Falling slowly.

...should give us time
To take the re-filled
Cylinders across
Before their gas supply
Runs out, and
Fetch the new churns
From the morning's milking.

On the tiny harbour wall
The cylinders are lined up
In formation
Two by two,
Awaiting their collection,
But of the milk
There is still no sign –
A hold-up we can
Ill afford.

Milk churns finally on board
We put to sea
To find
An alarming change of scene:
The wind already veered and strengthened,
So where lively,
White-capped waves had been,
Instead,
A heaving, threshing
Grey-green maelstrom
Lies between us
And our destination.

Beyond the shelter
Of the lee-shore,
We plunge head-long
Into the fray;
Foam flies
Along our length
Soaking passengers
With spray.

Uneven seas toss us now
And the bow
Meets unexpected breakers with a thud,
Juddering us from
Stem to stern;
Equipment in the wheelhouse
Starts to shift.

With one more monstrous lift
We meet freak waves
With a resounding crash;

A milk churn falls,
Shattering the seal around its neck
And spilling creamy gallons
Into the flooded bilge
Already swilling round the deck.
Suddenly,
The skipper brings his craft about
To meet the onslaught beam-on
And cuts the engine out.

The crashing stops.

First, we wallow, helpless,
In a trough,
Hemmed in by
Towering green
Walls of water,
Till we begin to glide
Sideways, upward
To the peak.

Through the icy rain
A brief glimpse
Of the distant lighthouse
And the harbour wall
Before the downward slide
Begins again, on and on
Through what must be
The indifferent sailor's
Idea of a
Living hell.

Driven sideways by the east wind,
We ride the swell,
Until at last
The worst is past:
The engine kicks in
And we can beat through
The remaining stretch,
To dry land.

With shaking hands
Ropes are made fast
By a pale and silent crew,
Chilled fingers fumbling
With the knots,
While numbed feet
Stumble up the
Wet and slippery steps
Which unaccountably
Refuse to keep
Still.

It has been a close call.

The skipper brings his craft about to meet the onslaught. Beam on!

Wind south west by south,
Force 2 to 3;
1020, rising slowly.
Good.

We heave-to
In order to retrieve
The orange marker-buoy.
Sudden, fresh-sea smells
Sharpen in the nostrils
As all hands heave
The gleaming lobster pot
On board,
Trailing clouds of
Deep-sea glory
In the form of
Streaming oarweed.

In fact,
This strangely active catch,
Violently self-propelled
About the deck
Contains no lobster,
But a very angry
And resentful
Conger eel.

Snapping jaws
Repel
All conventional means
To prise it from its lair,
But eventually
Half an hour or so

Of lateral thinking
Finds the monster
Writhing in the open air,
With everybody's fingers
Still intact.

Several hefty volunteers
Restrain the tail, while
The skipper
Separates it from the head –
After which baleful eyes
Still glare
And the threshing carries on
Independently,
Unabated.

The next step is to
Carve it into steaks,
And such is the life-force
Of the thing
That these, too,
Leap about the boat
For several minutes more,
Until at last,
All is still.

Hotel guests,
Relaxing in the evening
With a glass of wine
And a bowl of conger soup,
Have no idea
How many strong men
It took that afternoon
To persuade
Their starter dish
To come quietly.

iii Epilogue

According to reality
She left harbour
Many moons ago,
Superseded by
A fleet of
Fully-covered craft
Several times her size,
Whose stark,
Utilitarian lines
Come rain or shine
Complete the trip
In half the time.

Be that as it may,
In several other hearts
Beside my own
It seems
She is but temporarily
At rest:
Nestling in her cradle
On the Hard
Against a background of
Houses on a steep hill
She waits, until
On the stroke of eight
By the Town Church clock
She slips her moorings
In the early morning sun

Once again,
For her next cargo run
Back into our
Dreams.

Arrowhead

PRESENT IMPERFECT

CHILD GRIEVING

Here, then, is the dreadful thing
That I was not allowed to see before:
The gaping grave
Into which, this time,
Will be consigned
The remnant of my mother's
Spent mortality.

I only sought to confront
The reality of death,
Knowing with the instinctive wisdom
Of childhood
That this is how
You assimilate experience
In order to move on;
But the adults,
Imprisoned in their own fears,
And assuming
That I wouldn't understand
The truths they could not face themselves,
Forbade it.

There is a dreamlike unreality
In being with them both
Again
On an early summer afternoon.
Last time, I squatted on the sand,
Industriously manufacturing
Sandcastles,

While they sat motionless
On their
Ugly, grey, post-war
Utility blanket,
Watching.

In today's stillness
I arrange narcissi
In a marble vase for them
Instead; and when I turn to go,
This time
The wound will heal.

Industriously manufacuring sandcastles.

TO A NEWBORN DAUGHTER

Our eyes meet
Through the perspex of the
Comfortless aquarium
They tuck the newborn into
Nowadays

Raised on one shoulder and
Transfixed with curiosity,
You synchronise the movements of your head
With the hairbrush rise and fall
Of my weak attempt
To straighten out the aftermath
Of the battleground of giving birth.

At this pixel point
On your axis of unknowing
You are
The image of your own great-grandmother,
Wrinkled, plump and strangely capable –
And all of two hours old.

What have I done?
What wilful forging of another link,
Implicating you
In this lonely chain
Of giving and receiving pain,
The lot of mothers since the dawn of time?

In the small hours of your first night
I listen to the radio and watch you sleep,
Shrinking from what harm
I might unwittingly inflict on you
Before you come to lie where I am now,
And understand
Just how much there was
That I could not protect you from.

ALPHA MALE

I'm not suggesting
That you always meant
To abuse the power
You had; rather, that
You never truly understood
How being first-born, white,
Male and middle-class
Automatically admitted you to
The most privileged social group
On earth.

Together with good health
And superior strength
It was something you
Could take for granted,
Never quite realising
How complicated life can get
For the rest of us.

While I don't rejoice
To see you now
Made vulnerable by age
And failing senses,
I can't help feeling that
Somehow
It serves to bring you down
Nearer my level; so that
For once in my life
I stand a fighting chance
Of survival.

PASSOVER

Come -
drink of the stillness at my table:
with bread and wine and bitter rue
prepare to share my cup of tears.

Many who
dip into this dish with me
will betray, will betray,
and betray again. And yet,
down all the years
still I say: "Take, eat,
this is my body,
given for you".

And, while liquid notes of
haunting flute and
silver-washed words together fall
sliding into silence, even
as the slow drip of tears
once washed my feet,
do this in remembrance
of the greatest love of all.

TO A HARPSICHORD

There we are, then,
Yet one more examination day
Almost done and dusted.
Several Merits
And a possible Distinction
This time, I should think,
With no small thanks
To you.

I wonder,
When your keyboards are
Uncoupled,
Your pedals disengaged
And the velvet cover
Draped again across your lid,
A musical anachronism
Left to stand in silence
In the corner of
Music Room One –
Do you dream
Of ladies in outrageous hats,
With artificial beauty spots
On whitened faces,
Feathers fluttering in dalliance
With gentlemen in satin breeches
And powdered wigs?

I wish that I could organise
A masked ball for you,
So that your silver tones
Might once again
Sprinkle the surface
Of sophisticated small-talk
With glittering highlights,
Beneath a million candles
Of crystal chandeliers.

But all I have for you
Is another grade three
Descant recorder player,
And a chance to snatch
Two more minutes
Of brief glory.

POET BURNING

The Literati
Stroke their beards
And nod their heads
Sagely:
"The true poet
Must mirror
Our destructive reality
In order to achieve
Greatness."

Clarity
Is all that seems to be
Required of me:

I look deep into the stone
And see
Past the crystalline
Now,
Back to the chaos of
Creation
Carried in its
Collective memory.

I skim the surface of
The falling tide,
Straining to hear beneath
Suspended harmonies
Eternally deferring
Resolution,

A restless stream of strange,
Shifting patterns
Which make more sense
The less I try
To understand.

To bear fruit
In the face of
Blood and pain and fear,
All the destructive force
Of creative anarchy,
I *will* forge beauty
In this refiner's fire
Or die trying.

OVERLOAD

There is no room in my head
For any more music.
The mirror stares back at me
In surprised silence;
Only permanently knitted brow
And perplexed eyes
Betray
The cacophony within:
The jumbled mass of
Minims, crotchets
And semiquavers,
All of them crammed in
At the last minute
Like packed commuters
Forcing back the
Closing automatic doors
Of a tube train in the rush hour.

Threatened with
Another influx of passengers,
The iron band
Tightens round my head again,
And against a background of ferocious whistling,
I begin to register
The whole year's sounds simultaneously:
Every Sunday's
Organ and piano music
Weaving dreadful counterpoint with
Pneumatic drills, pumps,

Rumbling barrows of heavy, yellow soil,
And men shouting,
Until it seems my skull must
Split,
Spewing its heaving, bloodstained mess of melody
At my feet.

Instead,
Trapped inside my screaming head,
I watch the wind
Run its fingers through
The leaves of the
Flame tree,
Or lie motionless beside
Dark, green-veiled,
Mysterious water,
Soothed by the
Secret metamorphosis
Of tadpoles' quiet turning into
Tiny frogs.

The piano lid remains shut
And the flute is
Lifeless on its stand.
Faith is empty, God is dead,
And in my head
There is no room
For any more music.

POND LIFE:

i SINE NOMINE

Alerted
By the sudden burst of
Unaccustomed physical activity
As the cat went
Hurtling across the lawn,
I arrived just in time
To prevent him from
Pouncing on the
Panic-stricken creature
Found struggling on the
Hard-baked earth
Beneath the shade of the wistaria.

What I had at first mistaken
For some kind of
Large newt
Proved to be
The bright yellow underbelly
Of a terrified frog,
Already ominously
On its back.

It lay still for a while
And then
As I watched,
Long, slim fingers
Closed around the edge
Of a prematurely
Fallen leaf,
Drawing it
Slowly, wearily,
To cover up its nakedness.

After that,
It didn't move again.

ii THE FROG PRINCE

With a soft, dull splash,
It slithered from
The leafy margins of the pond
And landed at my feet.
Although I've thought it
Many times before,
I still meant it when I said aloud,
"You have to be
The most amazing frog
I have ever seen".

A dark marmalade-coloured suit
Was crossed with
Handsome chocolate stripes,
Which trimmed its legs
And marked a pattern on its back.

It listened courteously
While I pointed out
That a heat-wave in August
Is not a good time
For a frog to consider
Leaving home.
Then, as it held me in its
Thoughtful gaze,
I found myself drowning
In melting, dark,
Beautiful eyes,
And suddenly I understood
Why it was
That in the world of fairy tales

He would have had to be
A handsome prince
In disguise.

Politely resisting
My attempts to turn him back,
He set off clumsily
Along the scorching patio,
Resolutely set
On self-destruct.

There was no sign of him
When I returned,
But in the evening,
On a stone at the water's edge,
A flat, leather shape
Lay beneath what should have been
The protective shade
Of water-lily leaves.

Too exhausted
To make the final leap,
Handsome chocolate markings
Had melted into
The dark, burnt-orange of his
Splendid skin,
Before the sun
Consumed my prince
And dried him to a crisp.

It crossed my mind
That long before the human race
Conceived the notion of the
Throw-away society,
Frogs' lives
Must have come cheap.

TRAIN
On leaving the Vale of Glamorgan

A single
  hot air balloon
  hangs quivering above the distant city,
  all golden
  in the early evening light.

Train whistle
  gives a gleeful shriek,
  savouring the headlong gallop
  for its own sake.

The fair-haired girl
  with a violin-case and
  as yet unwritten
  Father's Day card,
  hurtles towards her destination,
  holding court
  incessantly
  on her mobile phone.

Yawning distance
  has already opened up
  between us and the wide river,
  light and space
  of the place where
  lives were linked momentarily,
  though there can be no
  belonging.

Fading sky,
  now backlit by a sinking sun
  is washed with wisps
  of high cirrus cloud,
  against which
  light brush-strokes streak
  ever-widening ribbons
  of dispersing vapour trails
  from homecoming aircraft.

In our relentless
  rush towards the long shadows,
  more balloons in silhouette,
  inverted tears above
  a darkening landscape
  hold a thread
  leading back to the bright day
  where we began.

Dusk now,
  and lights in windows
  welcome; or perhaps
  serve to keep the creeping dark
  at bay.

I would have hoarded the
  whole weekend:
  wild flowers on a windy hill,
  broad, almost empty river bed
  and low red cliffs at ebb tide,
  keeping them carefully in a
  box with the balloons
  against a luminescent sky.

But they got left behind
  on the train.

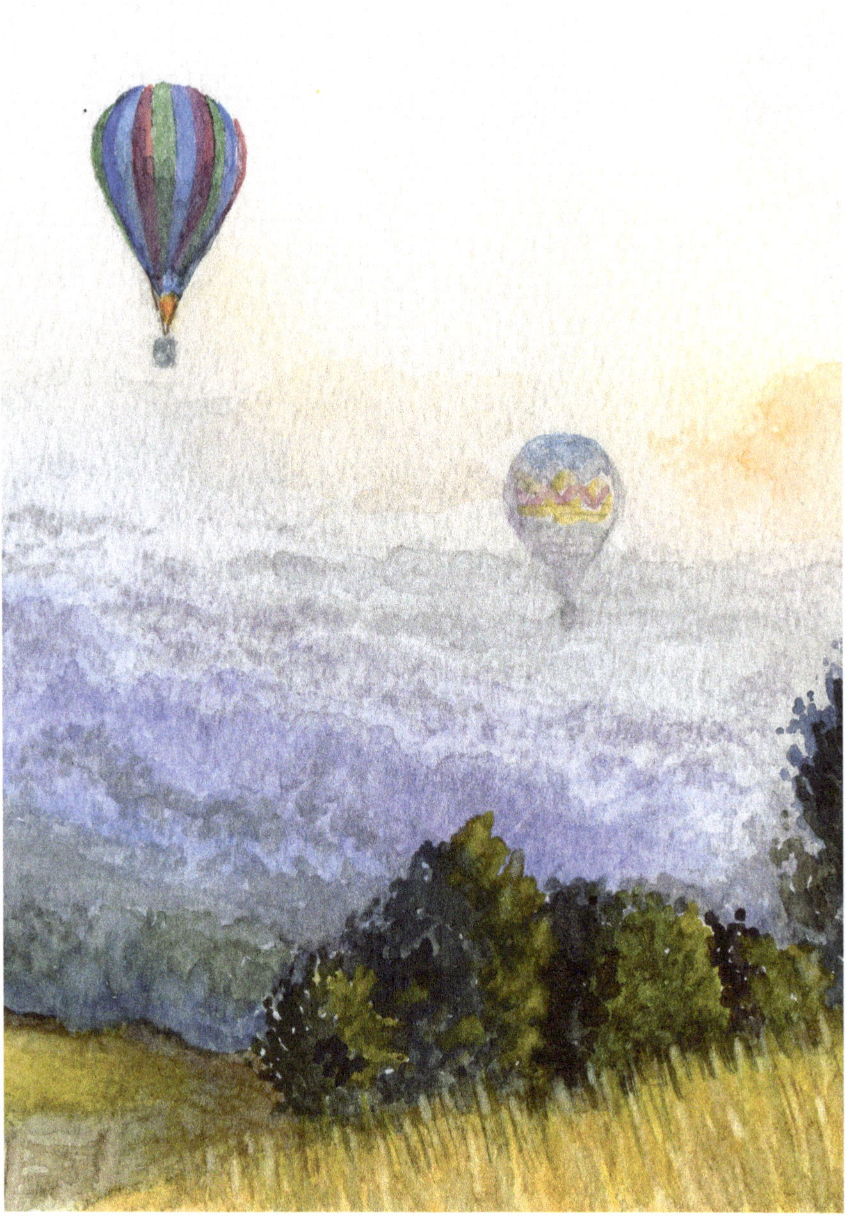

GIFT DAY

Today
Is a very special day,
A rare phenomenon –
No pressure,
No responsibilities,
Nothing looms
On my horizon
Clamouring for preparation.

Yesterday was such a gift
As well,
And I set out
Determined to be careful
Not to waste it.

While deciding
How to make the best of it,
I washed my hair
And watched an episode
Of an absurd
American
1970's sitcom on TV.

In the afternoon
A crossword puzzle
Occupied my thoughts
In waiting for enlightenment,
Until, after dinner
In the gathering dusk,

I wandered round the garden
In the rain,
Thinking that perhaps
I ought to have been writing
Something momentous.

Not knowing what,
I chatted to my daughter
On the telephone,
Discovering to my surprise
That disenchantment
With the current state of things
Is not exclusively
The preserve
Of the middle-aged.

Yesterday
Was a very special day,
But it can't have lasted
Long, because
Just as I began
To get to grips with it,
I found that it had gone.

DODECANI
Lassi, Kos

It seems so quiet
When the pain
Stops.

The outside world
Swims slowly into focus,
And from beyond
This bright Aegean room
With gold light fittings
And pools of blue shadow
In the corners,
The sound of wind
Tossing in the palm trees,
And distant motor cycles
On the coast road
Drifts effortlessly
Through the open doorway.

Framed by fluttering curtains,
An exploratory branch
Of bougainvillia,
Singing aloud
With flame-bright blooms,
Plays peek-a-boo
Above the balcony.

And when the pain stops,
Slowly
I come into focus,
In itself
A curious discovery,
Since I had more or less
Forgotten I was
There.

WHITE HORSES

Lassi, Kos

White horses are the same
The world over.

But, half a world away,
Grey minaretted pinnacles
Majestic on the skyline
Proclaim the mountains
Of the coast of
Turkey.
Giant supertankers
Beat past
The undulating urban sprawl
Of Bodrum,
Bound for Piraeus,
While a lone caique
Under light canvas
Runs before the wind.

Next to me in the taverna,
In a pushchair best described as
Battleship class,
An intrepid Viking baby,
Waving a triumphant sock
To the urgent cross-rhythms
Of the ubiquitous
Bouzoukia,
Adds an unexpected element
To the accustomed bleakness
Of an old, familiar scene;

Otherwise,
White horses are the same
The world over.

WILD FLOWERS

There is no such thing
As a weed;
For all creation is of
God,
And what we care to call
A weed
Is just a wild flower
Growing in the
Wrong place.

God is Love;
And if all love
Is of God,
I wonder if, somewhere,
He has a
Wild flower garden,
Where he keeps
All the love he finds
Growing in the
Wrong place.

A SONG OF THE WILD
Guernsey, west coast, early April

The wind-swept beach
Is empty, miles of sand
Swept clean,
In places ripped away
By winter gales,
To expose
Bedrock
Never seen before.

From a distance
Comes the muffled roar
Of breakers; far away
A solitary walker
Hurls a ball
Along the shore
And a tiny dot
Goes hurtling after it.

Planks are slotted
Into place
Across the entrances
To slipways
In the sea wall,
A small gesture
In the face of
That which is to come:

Before long,
In tree-hidden havens
Fishing boats will

Dance a mad fandango
Round their orange
Marker buoys,
While up on land
Taut stays
Slap against the masts
Of beached yachts,
And wind in rigging
Sings a wild song;

Sturdy granite walls
Will shudder at each
Broadside
From the driven tide,
While shuttered cottages
Hide behind
Their barricades of
Tamarisk and
Stunted pine;
Salt-sharp swell
Hurls its might
Right across the road,
Engulfing passing vehicles
And gracing gardens
With its calling-card
Of shining vraic[2]
And piles of
Polished stones.

---

2 wrack (Guernsey patois spelling.)

Long ago,
Despite uneasy fear
Of the unknown,
I had to see
What other worlds
Lay beyond
The safety of the
Harbour wall;
And although for me
The wildness
Would never be enough
To fuel a whole life's
Journey – even so,
Down the years
It is still the wildness
That I miss
Most of all.

FUTURE CONDITIONAL

SOLSTICE

It is as if for a split second
Earth stood still.
Day has trespassed into
Night's territory
As far as it can go –
And so, what now
But the age-old, gradual
Retreat into impasse, until
Time's protagonists
Stand shoulder to shoulder,
Equal but different,
Before the second half
Of the dance
Begins.

For what feels like eternity,
Life also stands still.
The morning post
No longer brings
External proof of self-existence;
Nothing left, then, but to be
An impotent bystander
To what now seems
Summer's hollow glory:
Peonies' short-lived beauty
Gone, crash-landed in the
Wet grass,
Their faded hue and cry taken up,
And perhaps surpassed,

By an inquisitive assembly
Of dignified sweet william,
Whose brief,
In shades of vibrant pink and red,
Is simply thus: to BE,
But in being,
Be beautiful.

If I could pray again, it would be
For a garden
In which to bear my own
Distinctive witness
In being what I am,
And not the slow,
Familiar decline into
Yet another long night.

IN SUSPENSŌ

In mid-ocean,
In the deep, black-velvet night,
Ours is the only light.

In reflections
From the cabin windows,
Seemingly we glide
On a strip of water
Barely wider
Than the ship's side.

Down below
On the bijou dance floor
Ageing couples strut their stuff
Beneath a glittering
Silver ball,
While nearby croupiers call
'Faites vos jeux'
To the inexperienced
Punters
Chancing their arm
At the crowded tables.

High above the rest,
At a cocktail bar
Near the crow's nest,
Ladies bedecked
In their best
Cruise-ship chic

Sip liquid of an
Iridescent blue
Uncomfortably similar
To the hue of
Windolene,
Topped with a cherry
And garnished with
A little paper
Parasol,

While the men-folk,
Awkward in their
Unaccustomed evening dress,
Bow ties
Loosened round the neck
And yearning for familiar ground,
Talk about the
Football scores.

But outside
The manufactured gaiety
Of these cramped floors
There is no land,
No sea, no sky,
No other friendly vessel
Passing by;
Arcadia blazes forth
Into a formless void,
Everyone assuming
That somewhere beyond
An invisible horizon
There will still be
Morning.

HARD WINTER

Cold air
Stings forehead, cheeks
And nose;
This year's buds
Taunt with half-awakened
Promise, needle-sharp
Against an eggshell sky,
While nearby
A wayward daffodil
Shows its tender head
Above the bare
Earth.

Beyond the hill
A slender, shy,
Misty moon,
Hanging low upon the chill
Horizon, glows
Opalescent in the
January sun;

Treatment's almost over,
Medication's
Nearly done:
On a day
Such as this,
Is it possible
That even my glass
May be
Half full?

BIRDIE DANCE

I woke before dawn
One morning in the
Early Spring
To a strange sight:

Along the shed roof
In the half-light,
Silent and intense,
A pair of blackbirds,
Swooping wing to wing,
And circling back to back,
Danced a
Private sarabande.

I advanced a hand
To adjust the curtain
For a better view,
But they had heard;
They knew
The spell was broken
And reluctantly,
Together
They took flight.

FLEDGELINGS:

i SUMMERHOUSE

Fledging time:
The garden,
Seething with activity,
Becomes a bustling aerodrome,
Flying lessons booked
The whole day through.

Yesterday
A well-drilled fleet of
Scruffy little coal-tits,
Fluffy, plumed heads
Still in 'punk' mode,
Flitted daintily from tree to tree
Behind their
Immaculately tailored
Parents,
Showing an admiring audience
How it should be done.

This morning was
The dunnocks' turn:
One hapless novice,
Beak still flattened
In its nestling's maw,
Peering helpless
From behind a
Loose panel
Jutting from the shed,
While a nearby sibling

Fruitlessly attempted
Vertical negotiation
Of the garden fence.

Now the blackbird
Martials his
Second tribe of teenage daughters,
Half-grown tails still rudderless
In flight.
A speckled chick
Gazes up at me
In puzzlement,
A bewildered mass
Of feathers
Dumped unceremoniously
Upon the lawn.

Never mind,
It won't be long
Before you get the
Hang of it.
This time next year
You will have
Found a mate -
Without the aid of
Social networking –
To dance your parents'
Stately sarabande
Along the ridge
Of my shed roof.
Together you'll have
Built a home,

Fed your family
The correct nutrition
According to their
Changing needs
And led them to
Successful adulthood.
Twice.

Unlike your
Human witness,
Watching from the summerhouse,
God has programmed you
To get it right
First time,
Without the need to seek
Professional
Advice.

ii YESTERDAY MORNING

For Lizzie, leaving for university.

Yesterday morning I sat in the train,
Letting the rain
Wash all my thoughts away,
Journeying over the rim of the world,
Flags unfurled,
Into the fray.

Now I'm expected to know where I'm going,
Intended to carve out a path of my own;
I'm not so sure that I know what I'm doing,
I think
I would rather go home.

All of a sudden the time rushes past,
Going too fast,
Running away with me,
Small and familiar the world that was kind,
Left behind
Yesterday.

Into tomorrow go yesterday's children,
Expecting to take the whole world in their stride;
Finding they're not quite as tall
As they needed to be –
And there's nowhere to hide.

Yesterday evening I freshened my face,
Emptied my case,
Put all my things away,
Tidied my childhood away in a drawer;
That was for
Yesterday.

SONG FOR ELUNED

and all daughters busy reaching for the stars

I watched a girl
As she danced by the water's edge,
Charged at the waves with the wind in her hair,
Raced with her love through the rock pools at sunset;
Long shadows leaping the sand –
Laughter that merged with the shrieking of gulls
In the sharp Autumn air.

One day there'll be
A boy and a little girl,
Gowns for a princess and trains on the floor;
Fresh truths to wrestle with, new skills to master -
All this and more
To add to the woman
She was busy growing into
Before:

O, lady Eluned
Your star is still rising,
Follow your dreams, you have time on your side;
Lady Eluned
My heart will go with you,
Though from a distance, and hoping inside... ... ...

You remember the girl
Who danced by the water's edge,
Cherish the girl with the wind in her hair;
Look now and then to make she's still with you –
Wherever life leads you, be sure she's still there.
Wherever life takes you,
Make sure she's still there.

SPRING CLEAN

Here is the detritus
Of a lifetime's education in
Being invisible,
Beginning with a
Hard wooden bench in a
Row of desks bolted to the floor,
Dreaming of escape from the
Stifling inheritance
Carved in stone,
While others more deserving
Were learning how to fly.

There in a heap,
No longer relevant,
Are all the things
Girls were supposed to want:
Waitress, typist, shop-girl,
Just to pass the time
In waiting for the
Wedding bells,
Followed by the Poet's
'Enemy in the Hall',
Spelling death
To creativity

But in this neat and tidy pile
Are the things
They said
'Girls like you
Can never do':
Paintings to finish,
Poetry to write,
All the music
Still to learn to play,
And the ministry
Not quite come to pass,
Always having been
A step or two ahead
Of the
Thinking of the day.

Nobody was listening,
All that time ago
And so many years
Have gone; but
The world already seems
A brighter place
Now I'm done.

STAINED GLASS WINDOWS

They had been conceived
As an entity,
And the variegated stripes
Of flamed copper
Organ pipes
Flared across the East window
Up above the casing,
To explode in a golden blaze of light
Cupped in waves of azure blue
Streaked with white,
A visual paradox
Of fire slowly rising
From a cascading sea.

The organist said
Suddenly,
With a quiet passion
Which I recognized:
"We have managed to create
A living landscape
Of colour,
Changing constantly
As the days move
And years turn,
Silent music
Which I hear as clearly
As I do my own."

I thought of other windows
I had known:
The stately galleon,
Dipping rhythmically
On the fresh, green morning tide,
Creamy sails spreading wide,
Rose-tinted
By a self-effacing sunrise;
Or sweeping regally away
Into the west,
While I, suddenly bereft,
Was left
To light lanterns
In the pools of shadow
Lying in her wake.

She sails serenely on,
Majestic still,
High above the heads
Of passers-by,
Although the ship
I helped to tend -
Ears and eyes strained
For subtle changes in the wind,
Ready to go about
With course re-shaped and
Sails trimmed -
Was almost lost
Upon the rocks named orthodox
By a misguided
And divided crew.

But latterly
My heart has learned to dance
To the strain of something new,
Another
Silent offertorium,
This time of
Jade green shallows
And cerulean blue
Of the fragile, upturned bowl of sky
Glowing now in glass
On high,
In a narrow lancet frame.

Repositories
Of shared memorial
To lives,
Not all recalled by name,
Which have already been,
Stained glass windows stand
Serene,
Mute witnesses
Who wait upon the lives and times
Which, as yet,
We have not seen.

OFFICES

This is not
What I would have wished
For you:
Such cramped quarters,
Your pictures over-large perhaps,
And just a bit too close together
On a wall
As small as this;
A far cry from the
Inner sanctum where
From time to time
Minds met
To catch a vision
And translate it
Into some new enterprise
For everyone
To share.

But this is your choice
And I don't have
To live with it.

It is not
What I would have wished
For me: perhaps
A different voice
Echoing from
That high-ceilinged,
Spacious room, now lined
With another lifetime's
Library;
No other mind to meet
Nor vision left to share
No smell of waiting coffee
Hanging in the air...

But this was your choice too,
Which can't be brushed aside
With 'I don't have to live with it',
Because I do.

HOW FAR IS IT TO BETHLEHEM?

How far is it to Bethlehem?
Not very far –
If you take
The shortest route,
That is:

Simply go to church
At Christmas.
It doesn't have to be
A full-blown
Midnight Mass
With all the trimmings;
Carols round the
Crib
Will do just fine.
There, you'll find the
Stable-room, lit
By a star,
Shepherds, kings,
And baby Jesus
In the manger,
Mother Mary
Tending him,
And Joseph standing
Guard.
With a lantern.

That's the
Christmas card version,
But it might be enough
To keep that
Warm, fuzzy feeling
Deep inside,
Until the pavement
Freezes over
And the next lot of bills
Come in.

How far is it to Bethlehem?
Ah, well,
If you want its
True meaning and significance,
That's a different matter
Altogether.

You see, the road
Doesn't end there;
It comes out
The other side
And continues on
Into the world beyond,
A lifetime's pilgrimage away,
Until it reaches
Golgotha,
Where, so they say,
The car park
Is never
Full.

THREE SOLILOQUIES
AT THE FOOT OF THE CROSS:

I am his mother, Mary;
I was there
The day they nailed him to the cross.
It broke my heart
That it should come to this,
But he always was my awkward one,
Right from the beginning:–
Angels, shepherds,
Wise men bearing gifts;
I think it was the frankincense
That worried me the most,
That was the real root of this
Life-long sense of loss.

We did our best
To talk sense into him,
Begged him to forget
This kingdom he kept on about.
We wanted him to leave
The crowd that he was mixing with
And come back home with us.
But he could be
So cruel sometimes:
"Who are my mother and my brothers"
Cut me to the quick;
I knew no good would come of it.

And now that he is dead
They say he walks abroad
About the land so changed
As to pass unrecognised
Among the closest of his followers.
As to whether I should know him
Now, I couldn't tell;
He hasn't come to me.

I am Peter. I was there
The night we waited in the garden.
"Stay and watch with me awhile," he said,
But, no matter how I fought
To keep awake, my heavy eyelids
Drooped with sleep, as if I had been
Drugged.

"Could you not remain awake with me
One hour?" To this day I hear
The accusation in his voice;
And how many times
In the stillness of the night
Before the cock crows, do I find myself
Back in that courtyard, saying to the
Servant-girl, "I do not know the man."

If I could live those days again
Knowing what I know now
About our risen Lord, I like to think
I could have been, no,
WOULD have been a great deal braver then;
But everything was so confused, it seemed
The whole world had come off its wheels,
And there was nothing left
Except to be afraid.

Of late, I have begun to think
There might be something habit-forming
About fear, that perhaps
You can learn to live with risk –
Become an addict, if you like.

Perhaps in years, or centuries
To come, it will be possible
To study what has happened here
And make some sense of it.

All I know is, since his death
Upon the cross, we have to see it
Through; this far along the road
Whatever future lies in wait for us,
There can be no going back.

I am Mary, called
The Magdalene;
I watched, helpless, as the life
Ebbed out of him: all his
Deathbed-raising, demon-cleansing
Chance to change the world
Evaporating to the sky.

There was nothing left that I could do
For him, once they had told me
Where his body lay, except to bring
The oils and spice myself, so that
I could be sure he had been laid out
Properly.

All I could think of as I
Hurried in the dark towards the tomb
Was, "How shall I roll the stone away?"
From the depth of tears and heartache
Who expects to find an empty grave,
And angels, shining bright, who ask,
"Why are you weeping?"

And then, - what joy, what disbelief,
The dead beloved
Risen and alive, exactly
As he said he would;
Forgive me, Lord, that in my grief
I took you for the gardener.

However hard for us
Believing might have been,
Blessed are those believers yet to come, he said,
Who have never seen.

HEAVEN IS BUT BEYOND
Church of St Francis, Valley Park

In the stillness of the
Autumn garden
Future, past and present
Press close together,
And I sit
Motionless,
Willing them to come to me.

Tall trees
Hold glowing arms aloft
To launch
Pentecostal tongues of flame
For a fresh
Coming of the Spirit,
While others bough low to strew
Dead leaves upon the ground
In a carpet
For the donkey passing
Yesterday.

And do you,
Blackbirds busy in the undergrowth,
Disport yourselves
At the feet of a St Francis
Only you can see?

If I look
Long enough
Will He give me
Precious glimpse of that
Bright Heaven
Which,
Being but beyond,
Is already here?

Summerhouse in Autumn

Earlier poetry books by Rosemary Parrott

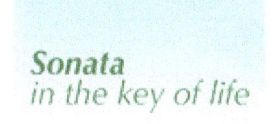

Sonata in the Key of Life
ISBN: 978-1-909054-01-1
Rosemary's first collection was published in 2000, and re-published in 2012. The poems are illustrated by Rosemary's own drawings

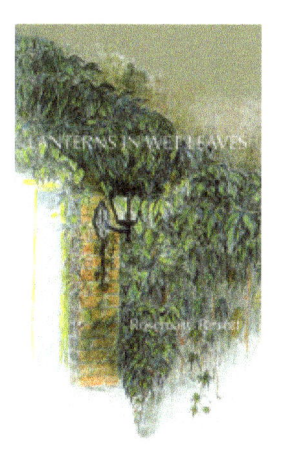

Lanterns in Wet Leaves
ISBN: 978-1-909054-02-8

Rosemary's second volume was published in 2012 after the success of her first collection. The books is illustrated by the poet's own drawings.

Milton Keynes UK
Ingram Content Group UK Ltd.
UKHW021628310324
440261UK00007B/91

9 781909 054363